Set Aside Every Fear

30 Days with a Great Spiritual Teacher

Set Aside Every Fear

■ ■ ■ ■ ■ ■ ■ ■ ■ ■ ■ ■ ■

Love and Trust in the Spirituality of

CATHERINE OF SIENA

ave maria press™ **AmP** **Notre Dame, Indiana**

John Kirvan is the editor and author of several books including *The Restless Believers*, and currently lives in Southern California where he writes primarily about classical spirituality.

For this work, early translations of various writings of Catherine of Siena, primarily parts of *The Dialogue*, have been distilled, freely adapted into modern English, combined, rearranged, and paraphrased into a meditational format.

Copyright © 1997 Quest Associates.

International Standard Book Number: 0-87793-624-2

Cover by Katherine Robinson Coleman. Text design by Elizabeth J. French

Printed and bound in the United States of America.

Library of Congress Cataloging-in-Publication Data
Kirvan, John J.
        Set aside every fear : love and trust in the spirituality of Catherine of Siena / John Kirvan.
                p.   cm. — (30 days with a great spiritual teacher)
        ISBN 0-87793-624-2
        1. Devotional calendars.   I. Catherine, of Siena, Saint, 1347-1380.   II. Title.   III. Series.
BV4811.K49   1997
242'.2—dc21   97-19240
                                                                                            CIP

Contents

With God as your companion
you will
live in the light of faith,
with hope and fortitude,
with true patience and perseverance,
all the days of your life.
You will never be alone,
never fear anyone or anything,
for you will find your security in God.

–Catherine of Siena

Catherine of Siena

As a blending of history and legend has it, Catherine of Siena

—was born in 1347, the twenty-fourth child of a reasonably prosperous merchant family.

—At the age of six, and again a year later, she had visions of Jesus and committed herself solely to him forever after. For the next six years she lived a life of voluntary fasting, solitude, prayer, deprivation, and flagellation, leaving home only to attend Mass.

—Marriageable at the age of twelve, she socialized for a while. But when her family picked a suitable husband for her, she told them of her spiritual commitment and shaved her head as a sign of her determination.

—Catherine persisted until she was reluctantly admitted to a group of lay women, widows who wore the black and white Dominican habit, who long before had caught her imagination.

She retreated to her room for the next three years and lived a life of solitary contemplation.

—In her early twenties she realized that love of God cannot be separated from service of humanity and she left her room for the streets and sick beds of the city.

—In the years that followed Catherine assumed a prison ministry that made her a familiar, desired presence in cells and at execution sites. She became "mama" to a host of followers, old and young, lay and religious, who welcomed her leadership and spiritual guidance.

—Catherine also exercised an innate skill for mediation, first in local disputes, then regionally, and ultimately at the papal courts of Rome and Avignon, where by papal invitation she worked to unify a divided church. She dictated hundreds of letters to church and political leaders as well as the most ordinary souls, praising, excoriating, urging, demanding, instructing, and consoling.

—During these years she composed and dictated her extraordinary work *The Dialogue*, a summary of her theology, her spirituality, her pastoral concerns, and her convictions—and became the first woman to be published in one of the Italian dialects.

And at the age of thirty-three, Catherine of Siena died.

Given such a life story to work with, it is easy to understand why biographers and spiritual writers have often sacrificed the woman and the mystic to the dramatic and the sensational story.

At bare-bones level it is hard to escape the impression that here is a single-minded, strong-willed, (stubborn?) woman, who from her earliest years knew exactly what she wanted and what God wanted of her. There is no evidence that she changed her mind about much, and it is clear that compromise was for her not much of a virtue. She was gifted with great imagination and contrary to expectations and custom, donned the garb of a religious order without ever leaving her parents' home for the life of a convent. She may have sought out strong spiritual directors, but she never submitted to a Mother Superior. Instead she surrounded herself with strong, committed clergy, religious, and laity, mostly male. No company, street criminals, or popes intimidated her. She may have been told that women were inferior, but she obviously did not believe it.

Such a personal history could easily make Catherine of Siena an extraordinarily fascinating figure, but also an unapproachable one whose life experiences have very little to say to the run of our humanity. Some would say, indeed, that critical aspects of her early spirituality are not only inimitable but undesirable, unusual to the point of being bizarre and so far removed from our sensibilities as to be examples of the very things that have given the mystical life a bad name. They can appear to our eyes more neurotic than humanly fulfilling, easily dismissed by twenty-first-century seekers as fourteenth-century spiritual aberrations. Too many readers stop right there.

The task of this small book is not to resolve such questions but to get behind and beyond the unusual and the dramatic and to provide access to the spiritual core that blossomed out of the early years to give strength and direction to the extraordinary final years.

To do this, we have chosen just one of a dozen possible images that Catherine uses to speak of the spiritual life. Here, we will focus on the image of the river and the bridge—the river that most of us dispiritedly slog through, and the bridge built over it for our safe passage. And we have chosen to highlight perhaps the most central theme of her insights and her career as a world figure—the irreducible connection between love of God and service of humanity.

Within the structure of this book we have mirrored her great insight that God does indeed speak to us, and that the spiritual life, in the end, is a dialogue of love between the God-who-is and we-who-are-not.

How to Pray This Book

The purpose of this book is to open a gate for you, to make accessible the spiritual insight and wisdom of one of history's most extraordinary women, Catherine of Siena.

This is not a book for mere reading. It invites you to meditate and pray its words on a daily basis over a period of thirty days and to enter into prayer in a special way through the unique doorway of Catherine's visionary experiences, her dialogue with "Sweet Truth."

It is a handbook for a special kind of spiritual journey.

Before you read the "rules" for taking this journey, remember that this book is meant to free your spirit, not confine it. If on any day the meditation does not resonate well for you, turn elsewhere to find a passage which seems to best fit the spirit of your day and your soul. Don't hesitate to repeat a day as often as you like until you feel that you have discovered what the Spirit, through the words of the author, has to say to your spirit.

To help you along the way, there are some suggestions on one way to use this book as a cornerstone of your daily prayers. They are based on the three forms of prayer central to Western spiritual tradition: the lesson, the meditation, and the petition. The author of the classic *Cloud of Unknowing* has written that "they might better be called reading, reflecting, and praying. These three are so linked together that there can be no profitable reflection without first reading or hearing. Nor will beginners or even the spiritually adept come to true prayer without first taking time to reflect on what they have heard or read."

So for these thirty days there are daily readings for the beginning of the day developed from the writings of Catherine. There follows a meditation in the form of a mantra to carry with you for reflection throughout the day. And there is an exercise for bringing your day to an end that asks you to find a place of quiet dark where you might enter into silence, as well as a final petitionary prayer at day's end.

But the forms and suggestions are not meant to become a straitjacket. Go where the Spirit leads you.

As Your Day Begins

As the day begins set aside a quiet moment in a quiet place to do the reading provided for the day.

The passages are short; they never run more than a couple of hundred words. They have been carefully selected, though, to give a spiritual focus, a spiritual center to your whole day. They are designed to remind you, as another day begins, of your own existence at a spiritual level. They are meant to put you in the presence of the spiritual master who is your companion and teacher on this journey. This is especially true of this journey with Catherine of Siena. The readings are her report of God's words to her, God's side of the dialogue. And since the purpose of the passage is to remind you that at every moment you are in the presence of a God who invites you continually, but quietly, to live in and through him, what better source than the words of God himself?

Do not be discouraged, however, if you do not fully understand the reading. Don't be surprised if you understand nothing. We have worked hard to provide easier access to her original text, but the words of great mystics like Catherine can be pondered for a lifetime without grasping all their riches. Understanding is not the point. Your heart's response is. These readings record segments of mysterious experience from the life of Catherine, clouded entries into the mind of God. With one exception, Day Thirty, they are passages in

SET ASIDE EVERY FEAR

which God is speaking. It may take time, perhaps a long time, for you to become comfortable with them. But in this thirty-day program you will be invited to do only what you can, to experience the Spirit in your own time and at your own pace. The effort required may prove to be exasperating, but it could also be unusually rewarding.

A word of advice: proceed slowly. Very slowly. The passages have been broken down into sense lines to help you do just this. Don't read to get to the end, but to savor each word, each phrase, each image. There is no predicting, no determining in advance, what short phrase, what word will trigger a response in your spirit. Give God a chance. After all, you are not reading these passages, you are praying them. You are establishing a mood of spiritual attentiveness for your whole day. What's the rush?

All Through Your Day

Immediately following the day's reading you will find a single sentence, a meditation in the form of a mantra, a word borrowed from the Hindu tradition. This phrase is meant as a companion for your spirit as it moves through a busy day. Write it down on a 3" x 5" card or on the appropriate page of your daybook. Look at it as often as you can. Repeat it quietly to yourself, and go on your way.

It is not meant to stop you in your tracks or to distract you from responsibilities but simply, gently, to remind you of the presence of God and your desire to respond to this presence.

You might consider carrying this mantric text with you in order to let its meaning sink more deeply into your imagination. Resist the urge to pull it apart, to make clean, clear, rational sense of it. A mantra is not an idea. It is a way of knowing God in a manner that emphasizes that the object of our search is immeasurably mysterious.

As Your Day Is Ending

This is a time for letting go of the day, for entering a world of imaginative prayer.

We suggest that you choose a quiet, dark place that you can return to each day at its ending. When you come to it your first task is to quiet your spirit. Sit or kneel . . . whatever stills your soul. Breath deeply. Inhale, exhale—slowly and deliberately, again and again until you feel your body let go of its tension.

Now, using the least possible light, follow the evening exercise slowly, phrase by phrase, stopping as its suggests. If you find your mind arguing with it, analyzing it, trying to figure out its meanings and goals, don't be surprised. Simply start again by quieting your mind and freeing your imagination. Put behind you, as best you can, all that consciously or unconsciously stands between you and God.

This exercise is not meant to last more than a few minutes. End it when you are comfortable doing so. It has two parts. The first, in keeping with Catherine's model, is a personal response to the words spoken by God in the day's reading. Just as God has spoken to you, so you speak to God. Second, you are invited to turn to the familiarity of a prayer based on Catherine's own words. It is an act of trust and confidence, an entryway into peaceful sleep, a simple evening prayer that gathers together the spiritual character of the day that is now ending as it began—in the presence of God.

It is a time for summary and closure.

Invite God to embrace you with love and to protect you through the night.

Sleep well.

Some Other Ways to Use This Book

1. Use it any way your spirit suggests. As mentioned earlier, skip a
   passage that doesn't resonate for you on a given day, or repeat
   for a second day or even several days a passage whose richness
   speaks to you. The truths of a spiritual life are not absorbed in a
   day, or for that matter, in a lifetime. So take your time. Be patient
   with the Lord. Be patient with yourself.

2. Take two passages and/or their mantras—the more contrasting
   the better—and "bang" them together. Spend time discovering
   how their similarities or differences illumine your path.

3. Start a spiritual journal to record and deepen your experience of
   this thirty-day journey. Using either the mantra or another
   phrase from the reading that appeals to you, write a spiritual

account of your day, a spiritual reflection. Create your own meditation.

4. Join millions who are seeking to deepen their spiritual life by joining with others to form a small group. More and more people are doing just this to support each other in their mutual quest. Meet once a week, or at least every other week, to discuss and pray about one of the meditations. There are many books and guides available to help you make such a group effective.

Thirty Days with
Catherine of Siena

Day One

◆◆◆◆◆

My Day Begins

GOD SPEAKS . . .

If you choose me as your companion
you will not be alone;
my love will
always be with you.

You will never fear anyone or anything,
for you will find your security in me.

With me as your companion
you will live in the light of faith
with hope and fortitude,
with true patience and perseverance,
all the days of your life.

I loved you
before you existed,
and knowing this
you can place your trust
in my love
and set aside every fear.

Enjoy my love,
live in me
and take from me
the light of my wisdom.

Confront the princes and tyrants
of this world
with my strength.

Take from me
the fire of my Spirit
and share with all
my mercy and my burning love.

You are not alone.
You have me.

All Through the Day

You have me.

My Day Is Ending

I RESPOND . . .

Be my companion
through the darkness of this night.

With your strength
let me confront
the princes and tyrants
of this world.
Let me borrow
the fire of your Spirit
and share with all
your mercy
and your burning love.

You have loved me
even before I existed,
and knowing this,
I can place my trust
in your love
and set aside every fear.
Amen.

Day Two

My Day Begins

GOD SPEAKS . . .

The only way to taste my truth
and to walk in my brilliant light
is by means of humble and constant prayer,
prayer rooted in a knowledge of yourself and of me.
To pray in this way
is to walk in the footprints of my Son,
uniting your soul with me by desire and affection,

letting me make of you
an image of my self.

My Son said:
"Those who love me keep my commandments,
and those who love me will be loved by my father,
and I will love them and manifest myself to them."
I know a handmaid of mine who was lifted up in prayer.
I did not conceal from her mind's eye
the love which I have for my servants,
but rather clearly manifested it.
Among other things I used to say to her:
"Open the eye of your intellect and gaze into me,
and you shall see the beauty of your humanity—
all the beauty which I have given to your soul,
creating you in my image and likeness.

I have clothed you with a wedding garment of love;
I have adorned you with many virtues,
by which you are united to me through love.
And yet I tell you,
if you should ask me who you are,
I would reply:
inasmuch as you have lost and denied your own will,
and are clothed with mine,
you are another me."

It is therefore true, indeed,
that your soul unites itself with me
by acts of love begun in truth
and nurtured in humble, constant prayer.

All Through the Day

You are another me.

SET ASIDE EVERY FEAR

My Day Is Ending

I RESPOND . . .

Be my companion
through the darkness of this night.

Open my eyes;
let me gaze into you
so that I can see
how beautiful you have made my humanity.
You have made me
an image of yourself.
Let me walk in the footprints of your Son,
uniting my soul to you
with desire and affection.

You have loved me
even before I existed,
and knowing this,
I can place my trust
in your love
and set aside every fear.
Amen.

Day Three

◆◆◆◆◆

My Day Begins

GOD SPEAKS . . .

You have asked me not only for suffering,
but for the determination
to know and love me
as the supreme truth.

Hear this:
to achieve a perfect knowledge and enjoyment of me,
the eternal truth,

you need never go outside
the knowledge of yourself.
It will be by humbling yourself
in the valley of humility
that you will know me and yourself,
and from this knowledge
you will derive all that is necessary.

In self-knowledge you humble yourself,
coming to realize that of yourself
you do not even exist.
Every creature, as you must learn,
is derived from me.
I have loved you and all my creatures
before you ever existed.
Moreover, through the ineffable love I have for you

I have recreated you in grace.
I have washed you in the blood
that my only begotten Son
has spilled out of a burning love for you.

Such self-knowledge will dissipate
the clouds of self-love.
Without the humility
that is born in self-knowledge,
no virtue can have life.
For humility is
the foster mother and nurse
of charity
and of all virtues.

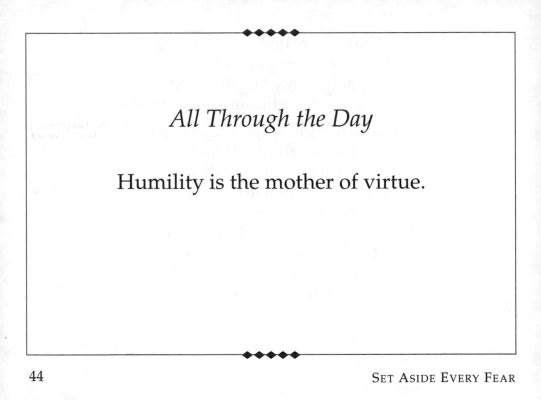

All Through the Day

Humility is the mother of virtue.

My Day Is Ending

Be my companion
through the darkness of this night.

Erase the fear
that comes from acknowledging
that of myself
I do not even exist.
Strengthen within me
the humility
that is born of this admission,
that is the foster mother and nurse

of charity
and of all virtues.
Without this admission, this knowledge,
my soul is lifeless.

You have loved me
even before I existed,
and knowing this,
I can place my trust
in your love
and set aside every fear.
Amen.

Day Four

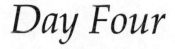

My Day Begins

GOD SPEAKS . . .

I want you to know
that every virtue and every failing
involves your neighbor.

Anyone who does not love her neighbor,
who does not help her,
who does not pray for her,
injures herself.

For to cut yourself off from your neighbor
is to cut yourself off from grace.
Unless you love me you cannot love your neighbor,
and to deprive your soul of love for me and your neighbor
is to do evil.

Love for me
in the form of prayer and desire
on her behalf
is a debt that you owe to your neighbors.

You are bound
to help one another by word and in truth,
by the example of good works,
and by responding in every way
to their need.

Tend to them
as you would tend to your own soul,
selflessly.
Not to love your neighbor
by depriving her of the good that you owe her
is to injure her,
is to do her evil.

This is a debt you owe to every creature,
but especially to those
who are close at hand.

All Through the Day

Love is a debt
you owe to everyone.

My Day Is Ending

I RESPOND . . .

Be my companion
through the darkness of this night.

You have loved
my neighbors
with the same love
that you have loved me.
Let me not forget them
here in the night,
but tend to them
as selflessly
as I would to my own soul.

To cut myself off from them
would be to cut myself off from grace,
from you.

You have loved me
even before I existed,
and knowing this,
I can place my trust
in your love
and set aside every fear.
Amen.

Day Five

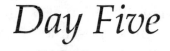

My Day Begins

GOD SPEAKS . . .

Loving me and loving your neighbor
are inseparable.

To the degree that you love me
you love your neighbor,
because love of her comes from me.
It is my gift to you.

Through the love of neighbor
that I make possible for you,
your virtue grows.
You prove that you possess me
by nurturing love of me
in the soul of your neighbor,
praying constantly for her,
desiring my glory
and the salvation of her soul.

Enamored of my truth
you must never cease
to serve all my creatures,
according to their special needs.
One you will help with words,
another with the example of your life.

To one you will show this virtue,
to another, something else.

There are in my house many mansions,
but love alone will gain you entrance—
a love for me
completed in
the love of your neighbor.

No matter what your state of life,
it is only by binding yourself to me in love
that you can love and serve your neighbor.

All Through the Day

Love me, and you love your neighbor.

My Day Is Ending

Be my companion
through the darkness of this night.

As this night begins
remind me
that I can possess you
only if
I nurture love of you
in the soul of my neighbor.
Hear my prayers for her.
Let them not end
with the passing of this night,

but be part of every busy day,
part of every prayer I pray.

You have loved me
even before I existed,
and knowing this,
I can place my trust
in your love
and set aside every fear.
Amen.

Day Six

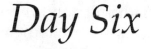

My Day Begins

GOD SPEAKS . . .

Your neighbors will bring out your true character.

In the good they elicit good,
in the wicked, evil.
The proud cannot harm
a truly humble person.
Nor can an unbeliever shake the faith
of someone who truly believes.

Their lack of faith will not diminish your faith,
but rather strengthen it,
if your heart
is rooted in love of me.

In the same way
patience, benignity, and kindness—
if they are real and true—
will blossom
in the face of another's envy,
anger, annoyance, and hatred.

Indeed, it is often true
that not only is your virtue proved
when you return good for evil,
but that when you reply to hatred and rancor
in another's heart

with the coals of your own fiery love,
their hatred will be extinguished.

Good can come from evil
when you respond to evil
with love and patience,
with fortitude and perseverance,
with endurance
in the face of those
who would turn you away
from the love of me.

All Through the Day

Virtue is for testing.
Respond to evil with love and patience.

My Day Is Ending

I RESPOND . . .

Be my companion
through the darkness of this night.

Let good emerge
from the evils I have met this day
and that await me tomorrow.
Teach me
in the silence of this night
how to meet them
with love and patience,
with fortitude and perseverance.
Let my love for you endure

in the face of those
who would turn me away
from the love of you.

You have loved me
even before I existed,
and knowing this,
I can place my trust
in your love
and set aside every fear.
Amen.

Day Seven

◆◆◆◆◆

My Day Begins

GOD SPEAKS . . .

Human hunger is insatiable,
far beyond earth's ability to satisfy you.

I have placed you above all creatures
and not beneath them,
and so you cannot be satisfied or content
except by something greater than yourself.

There is nothing greater than you
but me,
the eternal God.
I alone can satisfy you.

By sin and guilt
you can deprive yourself of this satisfaction
and remain unsatisfied,
in constant torment and pain,
weeping for what has been lost.

Self-love is a tree
on which grows nothing
but the fruits of death—
dead flowers, dry leaves,
branches bent down,

its trunk
buffeted by every wind.

You are all trees made for loving.
Without love you cannot live,
for you have been made by me for love.
The virtuous plant their trees
in humility,
sinners in pride.

Trees badly planted
cannot bear the fruits of life,
but only of death.

All Through the Day

You have been created for love.

My Day Is Ending

I RESPOND . . .

Be my companion
through the darkness of this night.

After a day filled
with needs and duties,
when I have been able
to think only of myself,
remind me in this quiet time
that you have made me for loving
that which alone is greater than myself.
Cut down the tree of self-love
on which grows nothing

but the fruits of death,
dead flowers, dry leaves,
branches bent down,
its trunk
buffeted by every wind.
Plant in its place a love for you.

You have loved me
even before I existed,
and knowing this,
I can place my trust
in your love
and set aside every fear.
Amen.

Day Eight

My Day Begins

GOD SPEAKS . . .

If you truly love your neighbor
you will feel within you
the fire of my love,
because love of neighbor
is developed out of love for me,
that is, out of recognizing
my goodness in you.

When you see yourself
to be ineffably loved by me,
you should understand
that you are to love
as you are loved,
that you are bound
to love every one of my creatures
with the same love
with which you see yourself to be loved by me.

Recognizing my love for you,
you will come to understand
that I love your neighbor
with the same ineffable love
that I have for you,
and you will echo that love.

You can in no way
repay me for the love I have lavished on you,
except by taking
the path I have given you,
serving me
by serving your neighbor.
I give you all my creatures
whether distant or close:
minister to them,
with the same pure love
with which I have loved you.

All Through the Day

Love as you are loved.

My Day Is Ending

Be my companion
through the darkness of this night.

When I see myself
so ineffably loved by you,
I need to understand
that I am to love
as I am loved,
that I am bound
to love every one of your creatures
with the same love

with which I see myself
to be loved by you.

You have loved me
even before I existed,
and knowing this,
I can place my trust
in your love
and set aside every fear.
Amen.

Day Nine

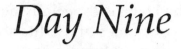

My Day Begins

GOD SPEAKS . . .

The sign of a lively faith
is perseverance in prayer.
The faithful soul
never turns back for any reason,
never leaves off praying
except out of duty
and out of charity,

for the Devil is especially active
in your times of meditation
and contemplation.

He wants your prayer to be tedious,
tempting you with words such as:
"Meditation is of no use to you.
Stick to vocal prayers."
He does this to tire you out,
to confuse you,
to tempt you to abandon meditation
and contemplation.

For such prayer,
when grasped by the hand of love,
with the arm of free choice,
and in the light of faith,

is the weapon
best designed
to defend your soul
against every enemy of the spirit.

Remember, therefore,
that it is by humble, continual,
and faithful prayer
that the soul acquires,
with time and perseverance,
every virtue.

Pray always.
Persevere.
Do not abandon prayer
because of the illusory words of the Devil
or your own fragility.

All Through the Day

Pray always.

My Day Is Ending

Be my companion
through the darkness of this night.

Here in the silence
I confess that I tire easily,
that at times
praying seems tedious,
even useless,
and I am ready
to leave your presence.
Don't let me surrender
in confusion,

but let me grasp with the hand of love,
with the arm of free choice,
and the light of faith,
the truth that I do not pray alone.

You have loved me
even before I existed,
and knowing this,
I can place my trust
in your love
and set aside every fear.
Amen.

Day Ten

------◆◆◆◆◆------

My Day Begins

GOD SPEAKS . . .

Prayer
that is only repeated words
rather than an act of love
provides little nourishment for the soul,
and precious little fuel for its passion.

It is not enough
to recite a psalm

or an Our Father
thoughtlessly
and then go on your way,
placing your trust only
in the repetition of their words.
By itself
this is fruitless.

Do I mean
that you should abandon
such prayer?
Of course not.

Your soul will grow by stages
and just as the soul is at first imperfect,
so too will be your prayer.

Continue
to pray with familiar words,
but join them to meditation.

While you are reciting them,
elevate your mind to me.
Recall my love
and your own imperfection,
so that
in this self-knowledge
you will recognize and respond
humbly
to my presence in your life.

All Through the Day

Not with words alone
do you pray.

My Day Is Ending

I RESPOND . . .

Be my companion
through the darkness of this night.

It is not enough, I know,
as darkness descends,
to mutter familiar words,
to recite a psalm
or an Our Father
thoughtlessly
and then go on my way into sleep,
placing my trust

only in the repetition of the words.
So raise my mind to you,
recall to me your love,
your supporting presence in my life,
the fact
that I have more than familiar words.
I have you.

You have loved me
even before I existed,
and knowing this,
I can place my trust
in your love
and set aside every fear.
Amen.

Day Eleven

My Day Begins

GOD SPEAKS . . .

From the beginning
I created you in my own image and likeness
in order that you might have eternal life,
that you might partake of me
and taste my eternal sweetness and goodness.
But the road I made for you
was broken so thoroughly
by the sin and disobedience of Adam

that no one could arrive at the eternal life
which I had destined for them.

The flesh immediately began to war
against the spirit.
All of nature rebelled against you.

A tempestuous flood arose
which to this day
buffets you with its currents,
overwhelming you with weariness
from the world, the flesh, and the Devil.

You could drown in that flood
because no one can arrive at eternal life
with only their own virtue.

But my Son has become a bridge
so that you may not drown—
a bridge
that stretches from heaven to earth
and constitutes the union
which I have forged with humanity,
with you.

All Through the Day

You need not drown. . . .

My Day Is Ending

I RESPOND . . .

Be my companion
through the darkness of this night.

From the beginning
you created me to your own image and likeness
in order that I might have eternal life,
that I might partake of you,
tasting your eternal sweetness and goodness.
But we travel by a broken road
on broken limbs.
I cannot arrive at eternal life
without your support.

I cannot go it alone.
Be my companion,
my guide,
my support.

You have loved me
even before I existed,
and knowing this,
I can place my trust
in your love
and set aside every fear.
Amen.

Day Twelve

My Day Begins

GOD SPEAKS . . .

I have made a bridge
of my Word,
of my only begotten Son.
He rebuilds the road
between heaven and earth
that was broken
by the sin and disobedience
of Adam.

If you were ever
to pass through the bitterness of the world
and arrive at life,
it was necessary for me to build a bridge
that would join your humanity
with my divinity.

It could not be made of human nature alone,
for human nature
would not be great enough
to repair the break
that was caused by the sin of Adam.

It was necessary for me
to join my divinity
to human nature
to create a bridge

and rebuild the road
between heaven and earth.

But be clear about this:
in order for you to have life,
it is not enough
that I have built this bridge,

You must walk across it.

All Through the Day

I have bridged heaven and earth.

My Day Is Ending

I RESPOND . . .

Be my companion
through the darkness of this night.

I stand as close to you
as my cautious heart allows.
I am here at the foot of the bridge
that you have built between us,
between heaven and earth,
between your divinity
and my frail, troubled humanity.
Reach out your hand.
Draw me forward.

Give strength
to my faltering steps,
constancy to my trust in you.

You have loved me
even before I existed,
and knowing this,
I can place my trust
in your love
and set aside every fear.
Amen.

Day Thirteen

◆◆◆◆◆

My Day Begins

GOD SPEAKS . . .

There are two ways,
and both are hard to travel.
There is the way of the river,
but there is also the way of the bridge
that I have built to cross that river.

How strange it is
that so many

still prefer to walk through the water,
even though I have built a bridge for them,
a bridge that offers delight,
where all that is bitter becomes sweet,
and every burden light.

Those who cross the waters of life
by taking the way of the bridge
see light,
even though
they are still in the darkness of their body.
Though mortal,
they taste immortality,
though weary,
they receive the refreshment they need
when they need it,
in my name.

There are no words adequate
to describe
the delight experienced by those
who choose the way of the bridge.
While still in this life
they taste and participate
in that good
which has been prepared for them
in the next.

You would be a fool, indeed,
to reject such a great good
and choose instead
to walk by the lower road
with its great toil,
and without refreshment or advantage.

All Through the Day

There are always two ways. . . .

My Day Is Ending

Be my companion
through the darkness of this night.

How strange it is
that despite the trust I profess,
I still so often
prefer to take the harder path,
battling dangerous currents,
risking the shoals
rather than crossing
by the bridge you have made for me.

Point out the bridge to me again.
Let me experience light
in the darkness of my days,
a taste of immortality,
a moment of refreshment
in your presence.

You have loved me
even before I existed,
and knowing this,
I can place my trust
in your love
and set aside every fear.
Amen.

Day Fourteen

My Day Begins

GOD SPEAKS . . .

I am your God,
unmovable and unchangeable.
I do not pull back
from any creature
who wants to come to me.

I have shown you
my truth.
I have made myself visible.

I have demonstrated the perils
of loving anything while excluding me.

But many still live
in a fog of misplaced loves,
knowing neither themselves
nor me.
They choose to die of hunger
rather than accept a passing
moment of self-denial.

No one can
go through life
without a cross,
far less those who choose
to walk without me.

Life is a tempestuous river
filled with treacherous currents.
There are those
who think they can avoid pain,
who care for nothing but themselves,
who turn their backs on me
and drown.

But I have given you a bridge,
my crucified Son,
that you might not drown.

All Through the Day

I have given you a bridge.

My Day Is Ending

Be my companion
through the darkness of this night.

You have shown me
your truth.
You have made yourself visible
and shown me what it is like
to love anything apart from you.

But in fact I still live
in a fog of misplaced loves,
knowing neither myself
nor you.

I choose to die of hunger
rather than accept a passing
moment of self-denial.

You have loved me
even before I existed,
and knowing this,
I can place my trust
in your love
and set aside every fear.
Amen.

Day Fifteen

My Day Begins

GOD SPEAKS . . .

Turn where you will;
you will find
nothing but my mercy.
I reach out
to all my creatures,
to sinner and saint alike.

To those who abandon me
in sinfulness

but return, I say:
"I do not remember
that you have ever offended me."

Imitate my love.
Pray equally for those
whose hearts have been converted
and for those who still persecute me,
that I may show them mercy.

My mercy
overcomes sin and death.
It gives light and life
to the just and unjust alike.
In the heights of heaven
it shines in the saints.

In the depths of hell
it tempers justice.
On earth
it is the language
with which I speak to you.

All Through the Day

My mercy is everywhere you are.

My Day Is Ending

I RESPOND . . .

Be my companion
through the darkness of this night.

Fill the silence with your mercy.
Wherever I look,
on every side,
let me see it
until I understand
that above all else
I am to imitate this about you:
I am to forgive
as I have been forgiven.

As I yearn to hear from you,
let others hear from me:
"I do not remember
that you have ever offended me."

You have forgiven me
even before I existed,
and knowing this,
I can place my trust
in your love
and set aside every fear.
Amen.

Day Sixteen

◆◆◆◆◆

My Day Begins

GOD SPEAKS . . .

If you keep in mind
my mercy,
you will not be mean-spirited with yourself
or with your neighbor.
On the contrary,
you will be generous
in your compassion,
nourishing your neighbor

with all that you have,
all that I have given you.

To act otherwise
is to be miserly.
It is to have a heart filled with avarice,
loving no one
except for your own profit.

The miserly
are concerned first of all
with their own reputation,
seeking constantly to take advantage
rather than to serve their neighbor.
The miserly
say one thing
and do another,

unable to enjoy the good fortune of a neighbor
or even their own.

The miserly,
rather than echoing my generosity,
take from those who have nothing.

The miserly
cannot sacrifice their soul
for another
because they cannot give
of what I have given them.

All Through the Day

Be generous with my gifts.

SET ASIDE EVERY FEAR

My Day Is Ending

I RESPOND . . .

Be my companion
through the darkness of this night.

I cannot find and possess you
by clutching greedily
to the gifts
with which you have flooded my life.
To expand them
I must give them away.
To possess you I must let them go.
My generosity
must match yours.
Everyone must trust my love.

You have loved me
even before I existed,
and knowing this,
I can place my trust
in your love
and set aside every fear.
Amen.

Day Seventeen

My Day Begins

GOD SPEAKS . . .

If you wish to rise above
a life of imperfection,
you must, like the apostles,
prepare yourself for the coming of the Holy Spirit.
Remain watchful
and persevere
in humble and continual prayer.

When you are ready,
my Spirit will come to you
as he did to the apostles
waiting in expectant faith
in the upper room.

You will be given the courage
to leave your safe house of prayer
and fearlessly
announce to the world
what you have come to know
of my truth and my love,
not fearing pain and rejection,
but seeing the glory
of whatever comes to you.

I will give you
a fire of charity
strong enough
to overcome your fears,
your love of comfort,
and all the temptations of the Devil.
Having the taste of my charity in your soul
you can arise
and give birth to it in your neighbors.
For you cannot love me
without loving your neighbor,
nor can you love your neighbor
and not love me.

All Through the Day

Await my love.

My Day Is Ending

Be my companion
through the darkness of this night.

Do not let me grow
too used to comfort and serenity.
Remind me that here and now
is only a waiting place,
and only when I am ready
will you send your Spirit to me
as you did to the apostles.
Give to me, as you gave to them,
the courage to leave
this safe place

and fearlessly tell the world
what I have come to know
of your truth and your love.

You have loved me
even before I existed,
and knowing this,
I can place my trust
in your love
and set aside every fear.
Amen.

Day Eighteen

My Day Begins

GOD SPEAKS . . .

Even the most worldly
render praise and glory to my name
because of my mercy.
My patient, abundant love
shines through them.

I give them time
to come to know me.

I do not order the earth
to swallow them
as a punishment
for their sins and indifference.
I hold back
neither my charity nor my mercy from them.
Rather I wait upon them,
commanding the earth
to give them light and warmth,
and the sky to move above them.
I bless their days
with all of my creation.

For even when they persecute you
for your faithfulness to me,
they serve me by bringing out in you

your deepest patience and charity.
Thus they turn their sinfulness
into my praise and glory.

I give my gifts equally
to the sinner and to the just.
Indeed it must seem that
I am often more generous with the sinner,
for I deprive the good person
of the things of this world
that they might better enjoy
the things of heaven.

All Through the Day

I give my gifts equally. . . .

My Day Is Ending

Be my companion
through the darkness of this night.

Fill these quiet moments
with your mercy.
Let your patient, abundant love
light up the night.
Bless me with the time I need
to know and love you better.
Do not hold back
your charity or your mercy from me,
or from any of your creatures.

Surround all of us with your light and warmth.
Bless us all—sinners and just alike.

You have loved me
even before I existed,
and knowing this,
I can place my trust
in your love
and set aside every fear.
Amen.

Day Nineteen

❖❖❖❖

My Day Begins

GOD SPEAKS . . .

I send my light
to give sight to the blind
and knowledge to the ignorant.
To the intellectual
I give an eye with which to discern my truth.

I send the fire of my truth
to consume their darkness,

to shed a light
that is beyond nature
so that even in darkness
they shall know the truth.
Even to the dullest mind,
what at first appears to be darkness
is now seen
as perfect light.

Because their minds
are endowed with my supernatural light,
and infused by my grace,
doctors and saints
have come to discover

light in darkness
and have learned how to turn darkness into light.

My truth,
I mean the Holy Scripture,
can seem dark
and beyond understanding,
unless it is read
by my light.

All Through the Day

That which is dark
becomes light.

SET ASIDE EVERY FEAR

My Day Is Ending

Be my companion
through the darkness of this night.

You are here,
you who by your very presence
can reveal
the light in every darkness,
can teach us how to turn
every darkness into light.
Send your light
to dispel the night,

to give sight to those of us
who walk blindly on our way,
and who journey without knowledge
of you and your love.

You have loved me
even before I existed,
and knowing this,
I can place my trust
in your love
and set aside every fear.
Amen.

Day Twenty

◆◆◆◆

My Day Begins

GOD SPEAKS . . .

Many who are well educated
cannot recognize my truth in scripture
because they approach it with pride,
blocking out its truth
and letting clouds of self-love
come between them and truth.
They take the scripture literally

rather than with understanding.
They taste only its skin,
never reaching its marrow.

They blind themselves to the light
which is found and explained in scripture.
They murmur that too much of scripture
seems to them gross and idiotic.

Because they have ignored and lost
my supernatural light,
and rejected my infusion of grace,
they cannot see my goodness
or the graces my servants
carry to them.

It is much better for the salvation of your soul
that you go to a holy, upright, conscientious person,
rather than to a proud, however lettered, person.
All such a one can offer you
is what he has of himself,
including the darkness within him.

You will find the opposite with my servants.
They will offer you
the light that is within them,
their hunger and desire
for your salvation

All Through the Day

Look to those who carry my light.

My Day Is Ending

Be my companion
through the darkness of this night.

In the silence of this night
let me hear and understand
the words you speak to me.
Do not let clouds of self-love
come between me and their truth.
It is not a matter of education.
Many who are well educated
cannot recognize the truth in scripture
because they approach it in pride,
blocking out its truth.

They find only themselves,
not your light,
but their darkness.
Help me find you.

You have loved me
even before I existed,
and knowing this,
I can place my trust
in your love
and set aside every fear.
Amen.

Day Twenty-One

My Day Begins

GOD SPEAKS . . .

It is necessary
to bear with others
and practice continually
the love of your neighbor
together with true knowledge of yourself.

Only in this way
can the fire of my love

burn within you,
because love of neighbor
develops from love of me.
It grows as you learn
to know yourself
and my goodness to you.

When you understand
that you are loved by me
beyond measure,
you will be drawn
to love every creature
with the same love
with which you yourself know
to be loved.

You cannot adequately
or directly
repay the love that I have for you,
because I have loved you without being loved,
creating you out of love
in my own image and likeness.
But you can repay me in my creatures,
loving your neighbor
without being loved first,
without any consideration
for repayment,
now or in eternity.

All Through the Day

Know that you are loved.

SET ASIDE EVERY FEAR

My Day Is Ending

Be my companion
through the darkness of this night.

In this quiet place,
alive with all your children,
draw me to them,
to love them all
with the same love
with which I know myself
to be loved by you.
Build a fire of love for you within me,
born in your goodness to me,

that cannot be separated
from love of
all those you have brought with you
into the silence of this night.

You have loved me
even before I existed,
and knowing this,
I can place my trust
in your love
and set aside every fear.
Amen.

Day Twenty-Two

◆◆◆◆◆

My Day Begins

GOD SPEAKS . . .

The desire
that you feel within you
comes from the love
that I have planted in your soul,
and it will never be satisfied.
The more, indeed,
that you love me,

the less it will seem to you
that you love.

Even when your body and soul
will be separated,
the desire
that you feel within you,
your yearning for me
and your neighbor's good,
will not end.

I have impregnated you
with my love.
You possess me
without any fear of ever losing me.
But your hunger for me

will never be satisfied,
will never die.

Your desire is infinite
and everything that proceeds
from that desire—
your love,
your tears,
your hopes—
become infinite
as they must be
if they are to reach me,
if they are to live.

All Through the Day

Your desire
will never be satisfied.

My Day Is Ending

I RESPOND . . .

Be my companion
through the darkness of this night.

Now in this quiet space I know
that you are mine,
that I need never fear losing you.
But my hunger for you grows,
so far outstretches my love,
that it seems at times
that I love you less than ever.
Let me be satisfied with knowing
that I will never be satisfied,

that my hunger for you
will never cease growing,
not now,
not even in death.

You have loved me
even before I existed,
and knowing this,
I can place my trust
in your love
and set aside every fear.
Amen.

Day Twenty-Three

◆◆◆◆◆

My Day Begins

GOD SPEAKS . . .

If you are a soul
without my light,
you are without my grace.
You do not understand
the evil of sin or its cause,
and therefore cannot and do not avoid it.
Neither will you know

what is good, what is virtuous.
Therefore you cannot love or desire me,
or practice the virtues
which are the instruments
of your spiritual growth.

Recognize, therefore,
how essential
my light is within you.
Without my light
you are walking blindly,
ignorant of vice
and the evil that follows it,
ignorant of me
and the life-giving virtues
that I bring to you.

You walk ignorant of your own dignity.

For sin is nothing more
than not knowing what I love
and what I hate.
It is loving what I hate
and hating what I love.
Living with this ignorance,
living without my light,
is the cause of all evil.

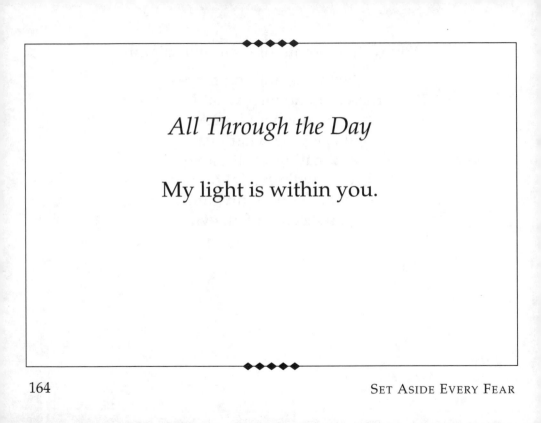

All Through the Day

My light is within you.

SET ASIDE EVERY FEAR

My Day Is Ending

I RESPOND . . .

Be my companion
through the darkness of this night.

I need not walk
blindly through the days,
hardly knowing the difference
between good and evil,
unable to love or desire you.
You have offered me your light
that I might be conscious of my own dignity,
loving what you love,
hating what you hate.

Let me not live in ignorance,
but rather
light up my soul with your truth,
my path with your love.

You have loved me
even before I existed,
and knowing this,
I can place my trust
in your love
and set aside every fear.
Amen.

Day Twenty-Four

My Day Begins

GOD SPEAKS . . .

In the pursuit
of spiritual growth
you will be tempted
to want the consolations,
but not the struggles.
It will be easy
to delude yourself into thinking

that this is not an act of selfishness,
but an attempt to please me more
by keeping me
more consistently in your mind and heart.

But it is a pathway to trouble,
designed in pride.

This kind of thinking
is not humble, but presumptuous.

I set the conditions,
the time and place
for your consolations and tribulations.
I determine
whatever is needed
for the salvation of your soul.

Never forget
that I give you everything
out of my love for you,
and therefore it is with love
and reverence
that you should receive my gifts.

Only by doing so can you grow.

All Through the Day

Receive my gifts with reverence.

SET ASIDE EVERY FEAR

My Day Is Ending

Be my companion
through the darkness of this night.

It is tempting
to ask you
to fill this night
and the days to come
with the warm comfort of your presence.
It is hard to let you set the conditions,
the time and place
for both consolation and tribulation,
for whatever is needed

for the salvation of my soul.
It is hard to surrender
to the love on which I depend totally.
But surrender I must.

You have loved me
even before I existed,
and knowing this,
I can place my trust
in your love
and set aside every fear.
Amen.

Day Twenty-Five

My Day Begins

GOD SPEAKS . . .

The sign that you
hope in me
and not in yourself
is that you do not approach me
and live your life
in servile fear.

If you are forever fearful,
afraid of your own shadow,
worried that the earth and the sky
will disappear,
it is a sign that
you trust only in yourself.
Dependent on your own limited resources,
you will spend your days
acquiring and hoarding
a host of worldly things,
putting your trust in them,
turning your back on me.

Remember that I alone
can provide everything you need

for soul and body.
Indeed I lavish my gifts on you
in direct proportion
to the hope that you place in me.

I am who am.
You are who is not.
You have received
your being
and every other grace
from my goodness.

They labor in vain
who seek to protect the city
that is not guarded by me.

All Through the Day

You are one who is not.

My Day Is Ending

Be my companion
through the darkness of this night.

For this passing moment I trust fully in you.
But too often
I trust only in myself
and I face the night and each new day
fearful of my own shadow,
waiting for the earth to open up,
and the sky to fall.
I spend my days acquiring and hoarding
a host of worldly things,

putting my trust in them,
turning my back on you, abandoning trust,
forgetting that you alone
can provide everything I need.

You have loved me
even before I existed,
and knowing this,
I can place my trust
in your love
and set aside every fear.
Amen.

Day Twenty-Six

My Day Begins

GOD SPEAKS . . .

You seek to suffer for your own sins
and the sins of the world.
But know this:
no suffering, no pain by itself,
can atone for even the smallest fault.

The guilt and punishment
that sin deserves
can be satisfied only by the desire of your soul.

True sorrow
is not in finite suffering,
but in infinite desire,
infinite love, and infinite grief.
Joined to boundless desire
and immeasurable love,
every pain, every suffering,
whether spiritual or physical,
whatever its source,
becomes infinitely worthy
and satisfies the infinite penalty
that sin deserves.

Inasmuch as your life
is filled with desire
and you accept your suffering

with desire and contrition,
your pain is worthwhile.
This is what Paul was speaking of
when he said:
If I had the tongue of an angel,
and if I knew the things of the future
and gave my body to be burned,
and had not love,
it would be worth nothing to me.

When, and only when,
our finite works are offered up
and seasoned with love,
do they become infinitely worthy.

All Through the Day

Suffering must be seasoned with love.

My Day Is Ending

Be my companion
through the darkness of this night.

At the end of this day,
I cannot offer you
prayers spoken with the tongue of an angel,
a soul gifted with prophecy,
a life martyred in your name.
But these things do not matter.
Without love,
they would be worth nothing to you.
You look not for infinite suffering,

but for infinite desire,
and immeasurable love.
I offer you what I have,
the little that I am.

You have loved me
even before I existed,
and knowing this,
I can place my trust
in your love
and set aside every fear.
Amen.

Day Twenty-Seven

My Day Begins

GOD SPEAKS . . .

The soul naturally
relishes goodness
though it is also easily blinded
by self-love,
and readily fails
to discern
what is truly good and valuable
to both soul and body.

The Devil will take advantage
of your blindness
and put before you
a banquet of his delights,
colored to look like something
that is good for you.

For each person he chooses
what is most appealing
to their principal weakness,
and to each according to their
station in life.
The Devil will issue you
an invitation to death
disguised as life.

He will attempt to snare you
on hooks baited
with the promise of pleasure and worldly success,
because only if you believe
that good awaits you
will you allow yourself
to be caught.

I speak to you this way
lest you choose death,
thinking that it is life.

All Through the Day

Beware of death masquerading as life.

SET ASIDE EVERY FEAR

My Day Is Ending

Be my companion
through the darkness of this night.

I need you by my side
through this night and all the days to come.
I am easily fooled,
I easily fall victim
to the thousand deaths
I mistake for life.

I need your help
to recognize the difference
between your gift of life

and the banquet of pleasures
life puts before me.

You have loved me
even before I existed,
and knowing this,
I can place my trust
in your love
and set aside every fear.
Amen.

Day Twenty-Eight

My Day Begins

GOD SPEAKS . . .

Do you know
what the special blessing of my followers is?
It is having their deepest desire fulfilled.
And since they desire me,
they have me.
They will transcend the body
and its laws which oppose the spirit

and all that comes between them
and the truth,
all that prevents them
from seeing me face to face.

In time
the soul will be free
of the body's weight
and its desire will be fulfilled.
Having desired to see me,
they will see me face to face.
This vision will be
their ultimate joy.
Seeing me they will know me,
and knowing me they will love me,
and in loving me

they will taste
my supreme eternal goodness.

This life,
this desire,
this possession,
this love,
this seeing,
this having,
this joy,
begins here and now
for those who desire me.

All Through the Day

Heaven begins here.
Heaven begins now.

My Day Is Ending

Be my companion
through the darkness of this night.

You have promised
that if I truly desire you
I will have you,
that it is possible
to transcend the body and its needs,
all the laws that oppose the spirit,
and all that comes between us and the truth,
and all that prevents us
from seeing you face to face.

I will hold you
to your promise.

You have loved me
even before I existed,
and knowing this,
I can place my trust
in your love
and set aside every fear.
Amen.

Day Twenty-Nine

My Day Begins

GOD SPEAKS . . .

Those who speak words of peace
all through their life
will at their death
receive what I have promised—
an eternity of peace,
of supreme, unending tranquility and rest,
an incomprehensible good,

the value of which
no one can measure.

I alone can value and comprehend
what joy awaits you.
The good that I have in myself
I will share with you.

I will not leave you empty,
but rather fill your eternity
with perfect happiness.

I await you
who come to me
with the light of faith
burning in your soul,
with charity aflame,

your spirit alive
with patience,
fortitude,
perseverance,
and all the other virtues.

I will keep
my promise
of eternal peace.

All Through the Day

I keep my promises.

My Day Is Ending

I RESPOND . . .

Be my companion
through the darkness of this night.

Put words of peace
in my heart
and on my lips
this night,
tomorrow,
and all the days of my life.
You alone know
what joy awaits the peaceful soul,
the good that you have in yourself

that you will share with me.
Do not leave me empty.
Bless my eternity with the perfect happiness
you have promised.

You have loved me
even before I existed,
and knowing this,
I can place my trust
in your love
and set aside every fear.
Amen.

Day Thirty

―――――◆◆◆◆◆―――――

My Day Begins

CATHERINE SPEAKS . . .

Eternal Trinity,
you are my Creator.
I am the work of your hands
and I know how deeply enamored you are
with the beauty of your workmanship.
O Abyss,
O Godhead,
O Sea Profound,

what more could you give me
than you already have given,
for you have given me yourself.

You are a fire that burns within me
to consume my self-love,
a fire that takes away the chill in my heart.

You are a light
that illumines my soul with your truth,
a light that ignites a faith
that is strong, constant, and persevering.

You are the clear waters of a sea
filled with sweet secrets,
a magic mirror
that you invite me to look into

to see myself as your creature,
to see you united with my humanity.

Beauty above all beauty!
Wisdom above all wisdom!
Wisdom itself!
Food of angels!
A fire of love to humanity!
A garment to cover our nakedness!
Sweet food for the hungry!

Clothe me with your truth
that I may finish my course
in true obedience
and in the light of faith.

All Through the Day

Clothe my nakedness in truth.

My Day Is Ending

Be my companion
through the darkness of this night.

I cannot come to you
with the soul of a Catherine.
I am only who I am,
a frail creature,
a tiny soul by comparison,
limited to words
that never quite capture
the depth of my longing.

I come to you
lacking in wisdom,

but filled with hope,
naked and hungry,
begging to be clothed, hoping to be fed.

You have loved me
even before I existed,
and knowing this,
I can place my trust
in your love
and set aside every fear.
Amen.

One Final Word

This book is no more than a gateway—a gateway to the spiritual experience and wisdom of a specific teacher that opens on your own spiritual path. It is an opportunity to join the dialogue between Catherine and God.

Now it is time to join Catherine in a final word of thanks for God's company on the journey we have shared.

Thank you, eternal Father, thank you.
You have not abandoned the work of your hands.
You have not turned your face from me,
nor looked down on my feelings.
You who are light, have accepted my darkness.

You the great physician, have healed my infirmities.
You who are life, have not left me to die.
You who are wisdom, have not been put off by my follies.
You have rather surrounded me
with your goodness and your gentle mercy,
and nourished in me
a love for you and for my neighbor.
Thank you, eternal Father, thank you.
Amen.

SET ASIDE EVERY FEAR